THE
ABSOLUTE
MADMAN

Tweets Authored by @realDonaldTrump on https://twitter.com

Printed in the United States of America

The Absolute Madman:

A Compilation of Tweets from President Donald Trump's Twitter Account

By Yosef

To everyone Making Earth Great Again

INTRODUCTION

THE TWEETS ARE IN CHRONOLOGICAL ORDER AND SEPARATED INTO 2 PARTS; PRE-ANNOUNCEMENT AND POST-ANNOUNCEMENT, REFERRING TO WHEN DONALD J. TRUMP ANNOUNCED HIS CAMPAIGN FOR PRESIDENCY.

SINCE THE DIGITAL REALM IS EVER-CHANGING, TWITTER STATISTICS SUCH AS LIKES AND RETWEETS WILL HAVE LIKELY CHANGED SINCE THIS PUBLICATION.

CONTENTS

PRE-ANNOUNCEMENT

Donald J. Trump ✔
@realDonaldTrump

Barney Frank looked disgusting--nipples protruding--in his blue shirt before Congress. Very very disrespectful.

3:36 PM · Dec 21, 2011

14,827 RETWEETS   **16,833** LIKES

Donald J. Trump ✔
@realDonaldTrump

What a convenient mistake: @BarackObama issued a statement for Kwanza but failed to issue one for Christmas.

Obama Skips Christmas Statement But Issues Statement for Fake Holiday Kwanzaa
thegatewaypundit.com

15

Donald J. Trump ✓
@realDonaldTrump

Let's take a closer look at that birth certificate. @BarackObama was described in 2003 as being "born in Kenya." bit.ly/Klc9Uu

3:31 PM · May 18, 2012

765 RETWEETS   **476** LIKES

Donald J. Trump ✓
@realDonaldTrump

With @BarackObama listing himself as "Born in Kenya" in 1999http://bit.ly/JaHQW0 HI laws allowed him to produce a fake certificate. #SCAM

10:07 AM · Jul 20, 2012

426 RETWEETS **141** LIKES

19

Donald J. Trump ✓
@realDonaldTrump

.@ariannahuff is unattractive both inside and out. I fully
understand why her former husband left her for a man- he made
a good decision.

10:54 AM · Aug 28, 2012

8,414 RETWEETS   **7,200** LIKES

21

Donald J. Trump ✓
@realDonaldTrump

Wake Up America! See article: "Israeli Science: Obama Birth
Certificate is a Fake"

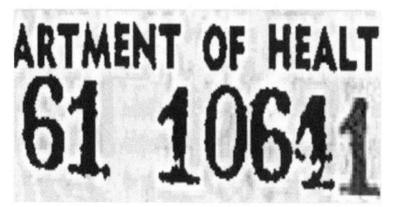

Israeli Science: Obama Birth Certificate Is A Fake - Freedom Outpost
freedomoutpost.com

11:40 AM · Sep 13, 2012

1,202 RETWEETS   **526** LIKES

23

Donald J. Trump ✓
@realDonaldTrump

I have never seen a thin person drinking Diet Coke.

2:43 PM · Oct 14, 2012

89,802 RETWEETS   **90,701** LIKES

Donald J. Trump ✓
@realDonaldTrump

The Coca Cola company is not happy with me--that's okay, I'll still keep drinking that garbage.

1:47 PM · Oct 16, 2012

19,542 RETWEETS   **24,468** LIKES

Donald J. Trump ✔
@realDonaldTrump

.@antbaxter Your documentary died many deaths. You have, in my opinion, zero talent.

11:10 AM · Oct 16, 2012

46 RETWEETS   **33** LIKES

29

Donald J. Trump ✔
@realDonaldTrump

Remember, I said Derek don't sell your Trump World Tower apartment...its been lucky for you. The day after he sold it, he broke his foot.

9:54 AM · Oct 17, 2012

389 RETWEETS   **115** LIKES

Donald J. Trump ✓
@realDonaldTrump

My twitter has become so powerful that I can actually make my
enemies tell the truth.

11:06 AM · Oct 17, 2012

7,684 RETWEETS   **8,724** LIKES

Donald J. Trump @realDonaldTrump   Oct 18, 2012
Hey @Rosie--how is your recovery going? I hope you are doing well
so we can start fighting again soon!

↩   ↻ 465   ♥ 633   ✉

ROSIE @Rosie   Oct 18, 2012
@realDonaldTrump - not well enough yet Donnie - I am sure Kristen
Stewart is having heart palpitations from ur latest outburst thx4caring

↩   ↻ 46   ♥ 69   ✉

↩ in reply to @Rosie

Donald J. Trump ✓
@realDonaldTrump

@Rosie @realDonaldTrump Thanks for the info Rosie--get well.

10:25 AM · Oct 19, 2012

48 RETWEETS   **124** LIKES

Donald J. Trump ✔
@realDonaldTrump

Everyone knows I am right that Robert Pattinson should dump
Kristen Stewart. In a couple of years, he will thank me. Be smart,
Robert.

4:48 PM · Oct 22, 2012

55,261 RETWEETS   **61,069** LIKES

Donald J. Trump ✓
@realDonaldTrump

.@BetteMidler talks about my hair but I'm not allowed to talk about her ugly face or body --- so I won't. Is this a double standard?

11:57 AM · Oct 28, 2012

2,035 RETWEETS   **1,424** LIKES

39

Donald J. Trump ✔
@realDonaldTrump

I will start reviewing various political reporters etc & websites as to their professionalism & fairness—many people asking for this.

10:46 AM · Nov 2, 2012

417 RETWEETS   **224** LIKES

Donald J. Trump ✔
@realDonaldTrump

The concept of global warming was created by and for the Chinese in order to make U.S. manufacturing non-competitive.

2:15 PM · Nov 6, 2012

104,929 RETWEETS   **66,995** LIKES

Donald J. Trump ✔
@realDonaldTrump

Why is Obama playing basketball today? That is why our country is in trouble!

9:48 AM · Nov 6, 2012

4,903 RETWEETS   **2,191** LIKES

Donald J. Trump ✓
@realDonaldTrump

Pervert alert. @RepWeiner is back on twitter. All girls under the age of 18, block him immediately.

3:32 PM · Nov 7, 2012

13,010 RETWEETS   **13,764** LIKES

Donald J. Trump ✓
@realDonaldTrump

.@cher--I don't wear a "rug"—it's mine. And I promise not to talk about your massive plastic surgeries that didn't work.

3:23 PM · Nov 13, 2012

3,494 RETWEETS   **3,733** LIKES

49

Donald J. Trump ✔
@realDonaldTrump

Dopey @Lord_Sugar—Look in the mirror and thank the real Lord that Donald Trump exists. You are nothing!

5:08 PM · Dec 6, 2012

597 RETWEETS   **366** LIKES

51

Donald J. Trump @realDonaldTrump   Dec 10, 2012
Dopey Sugar—@Lord_Sugar Isn't it sad that my golf course in
Scotland just got "best new course in the world"—it's worth more than
you are!

    ↰   ↻ 739   ♥ 728   ✉

Lord Sugar @Lord_Sugar   Dec 10, 2012
@realDonaldTrump How can it be voted best golf course in the world
if it is not open . You deluded idiot .

    ↰   ↻ 695   ♥ 509   ✉

↰ in reply to @Lord_Sugar

Donald J. Trump ✅
@realDonaldTrump

@Lord_Sugar Dopey Sugar--because it was open all season long-
-you can't play golf in the snow, you stupid ass.

1:13 PM · Dec 10, 2012

2,881 RETWEETS   **3,577** LIKES

53

Donald J. Trump ✓
@realDonaldTrump

.@billmaher was so nervous talking about me on the @jayleno show—I've never seen him like that!

11:15 AM · Jan 9, 2013

46 RETWEETS   **43** LIKES

Donald J. Trump ✔
@realDonaldTrump

I have accepted @billmaher's $5 million offer paid to me for charity (made on the @jayleno show).

12:59 PM · Jan 9, 2013

109 RETWEETS   **57** LIKES

Donald J. Trump ✓
@realDonaldTrump

Golf match? I've won 18 Club Championships including this weekend. @mcuban swings like a little girl with no power or talent. Mark's a loser

7:07 AM · Mar 19, 2013

1,415 RETWEETS   **1,450** LIKES

Donald J. Trump ✔
@realDonaldTrump

NO MERCY TO TERRORISTS you dumb bastards!

11:47 AM · Apr 21, 2013

17,559 RETWEETS   **21,354** LIKES

Donald J. Trump ✔
@realDonaldTrump

I know some of you may think I'm tough and harsh but actually I'm a very compassionate person (with a very high IQ) with strong common sense

10:05 AM · Apr 21, 2013

7,180 RETWEETS   **6,609** LIKES

63

Donald J. Trump ✓
@realDonaldTrump

Sorry losers and haters, but my I.Q. is one of the highest -and you all know it! Please don't feel so stupid or insecure,it's not your fault

9:37 PM · May 8, 2013

71,225 RETWEETS   **66,609** LIKES

Donald J. Trump ✓
@realDonaldTrump

How amazing, the State Health Director who verified copies of
Obama's "birth certificate" died in plane crash today. All others
lived

4:32 PM · Dec 12, 2013

7,380 RETWEETS   **5,372** LIKES

Donald J. Trump ✓
@realDonaldTrump

I hope we never find life on other planets because there's no
doubt that the U.S. Government will start sending them money!

9:59 AM · Jun 4, 2014

3,510 RETWEETS   **4,350** LIKES

Donald J. Trump ✔
@realDonaldTrump

Rosie is crude, rude, obnoxious and dumb - other than that I like her very much!

7:07 AM · Jul 11, 2014

421 RETWEETS **663** LIKES

Donald J. Trump ✓
@realDonaldTrump

If Obama resigns from office NOW, thereby doing a great service to the country—I will give him free lifetime golf at any one of my courses!

5:22 PM · Sep 10, 2014

30,821 RETWEETS   **35,281** LIKES

73

Donald J. Trump ✓
@realDonaldTrump

"@futureicon: @pinksugar61 Obama also fabricated his own birth certificate after being pressured to produce one by @realDonaldTrump"

5:53 PM · Nov 23, 2014

393 RETWEETS   **181** LIKES

75

Donald J. Trump ✔
@realDonaldTrump

Dummy Bill Maher did an advertisement for the failing New York Times where the picture of him is very sad-he looks pathetic, bloated & gone!

10:09 PM · Dec 23, 2014

114 Retweets   **196** Likes

Donald J. Trump ✓
@realDonaldTrump

I would like to wish everyone, including all haters and losers (of
which, sadly, there are many) a truly happy and enjoyable
Memorial Day!

4:26 PM · May 24, 2015

8,550 RETWEETS   **11,026** LIKES

POST-ANNOUNCEMENT

Donald J. Trump ✓
@realDonaldTrump

I just realized that if you listen to Carly Fiorina for more than ten minutes straight, you develop a massive headache. She has zero chance!

3:06 PM · Aug 9, 2015 from New Jersey, USA

4,007 RETWEETS   **8,734** LIKES

Donald J. Trump ✓
@realDonaldTrump

Truly weird Senator Rand Paul of Kentucky reminds me of a
spoiled brat without a properly functioning brain. He was terrible
at DEBATE!

8:41 PM · Aug 10, 2015 from Manhattan, NY

2,691 RETWEETS   **5,647** LIKES

85

Donald J. Trump ✓
@realDonaldTrump

"@codyave: @drudgereport @BreitbartNews @Writeintrump
"You Can't Stump the Trump" youtube.com/watch?v=MKH6PA... "

4:53 AM · Oct 13, 2015

8,274 RETWEETS   **11,353** LIKES

Donald J. Trump ✔
@realDonaldTrump

I have watched sloppy Graydon Carter fail and close Spy Magazine and now am watching him fail at @VanityFair Magazine. He is a total loser!

6:47 PM · Nov 15, 2015

787 Retweets   **2,113** Likes

89

Donald J. Trump ✔
@realDonaldTrump

Highly untalented Wash Post blogger, Jennifer Rubin, a real
dummy, never writes fairly about me. Why does Wash Post have
low IQ people?

3:46 PM · Dec 1, 2015

1,655 RETWEETS   **4,122** LIKES

91

Donald J. Trump ✓
@realDonaldTrump

Dopey Prince @Alwaleed_Talal wants to control our U.S.
politicians with daddy's money. Can't do it when I get elected.
#Trump2016

10:53 PM · Dec 11, 2015

12,124 RETWEETS   **14,555** LIKES

93

Donald J. Trump ✔
@realDonaldTrump

I am in Iowa watching all of these phony T.V. ads by the other candidates. All bull, politicians are all talk and no action-it won't happen!

10:01 AM · Jan 23, 2016

2,341 RETWEETS **7,598** LIKES

Donald J. Trump ✓
@realDonaldTrump

I wonder if President Obama would have attended the funeral of Justice Scalia if it were held in a Mosque? Very sad that he did not go!

11:42 AM · Feb 20, 2016

12,246 RETWEETS   **29,570** LIKES

97

Donald J. Trump ✓
@realDonaldTrump

Mitt Romney, who was one of the dumbest and worst candidates in the history of Republican politics, is now pushing me on tax returns. Dope!

7:34 AM · Feb 25, 2016

8,058 RETWEETS   **22,118** LIKES

Donald J. Trump ✔
@realDonaldTrump

I am watching two clown announcers on @FoxNews as they try to build up failed presidential candidate #LittleMarco. Fox News is in the bag!

1:09 PM · Mar 5, 2016

4,409 Retweets   **12,806** Likes

Donald J. Trump ✓
@realDonaldTrump

It is amazing how often I am right, only to be criticized by the media. Illegal immigration, take the oil, build the wall, Muslims, NATO!

10:38 AM · Mar 24, 2016

7,345 RETWEETS   **21,832** LIKES

Donald J. Trump ✔
@realDonaldTrump

How long did it take your staff of 823 people to think that up--
and where are your 33,000 emails that you deleted?

> **Hillary Clinton** @HillaryClinton
> Delete your account. twitter.com/realDonaldTrum...

4:40 PM · Jun 9, 2016

166,292 RETWEETS   **294,140** LIKES

Donald J. Trump ✅
@realDonaldTrump

Obama just endorsed Crooked Hillary. He wants four more years of Obama—but nobody else does!

2:22 PM · Jun 9, 2016

35,988 RETWEETS   **83,421** LIKES

Donald J. Trump ✔
@realDonaldTrump

Just arrived in Scotland. Place is going wild over the vote. They took their country back, just like we will take America back. No games!

5:21 AM · Jun 24, 2016

17,139 Retweets   **46,855** Likes

Donald J. Trump ✓
@realDonaldTrump

Other than a small group of people who have suffered massive and embarrassing losses, the party is VERY united. Great love in the arena!

10:49 AM · Jul 21, 2016

9,291 RETWEETS   **37,583** LIKES

Donald J. Trump ✔
@realDonaldTrump

Leaked e-mails of DNC show plans to destroy Bernie Sanders.
Mock his heritage and much more. On-line from Wikileakes, really
vicious. RIGGED

6:55 AM · Jul 23, 2016

23,613 RETWEETS   **52,418** LIKES

Donald J. Trump ✔
@realDonaldTrump

An analysis showed that Bernie Sanders would have won the
Democratic nomination if it were not for the Super Delegates.

8:30 AM · Jul 24, 2016

10,834 RETWEETS   **28,665** LIKES

Donald J. Trump ✓
@realDonaldTrump

Sad to watch Bernie Sanders abandon his revolution. We welcome all voters who want to fix our rigged system and bring back our jobs.

11:04 PM · Jul 25, 2016

23,043 RETWEETS   **66,827** LIKES

 **Donald J. Trump** ✓
@realDonaldTrump

Some day, when things calm down, I'll tell the real story of @JoeNBC and his very insecure long-time girlfriend, @morningmika. Two clowns!

7:29 AM · Aug 22, 2016

9,210 Retweets   **24,461** Likes

Donald J. Trump ✓
@realDonaldTrump

For those few people knocking me for tweeting at three o'clock in the morning, at least you know I will be there, awake, to answer the call!

2:37 PM · Sep 30, 2016

40,923 RETWEETS   **107,486** LIKES

Donald J. Trump ✓
@realDonaldTrump

The polls are close so Crooked Hillary is getting out of bed and will campaign tomorrow.Why did she hammer 13 devices and acid-wash e-mails?

7:17 PM · Sep 4, 2016

14,008 RETWEETS   **35,469** LIKES

Donald J. Trump ✓
@realDonaldTrump

Disloyal R's are far more difficult than Crooked Hillary. They come at you from all sides. They don't know how to win - I will teach them!

10:48 AM · Oct 11, 2016

21,815 RETWEETS   **55,948** LIKES

Donald J. Trump ✓
@realDonaldTrump

It is so nice that the shackles have been taken off me and I can now fight for America the way I want to.

10:00 AM · Oct 11, 2016

24,298 RETWEETS   **65,127** LIKES

Donald J. Trump ✓
@realDonaldTrump

Wow, @CNN Town Hall questions were given to Crooked Hillary Clinton in advance of big debates against Bernie Sanders. Hillary & CNN FRAUD!

7:04 PM · Oct 11, 2016

29,407 RETWEETS   **61,061** LIKES

Donald J. Trump ✓
@realDonaldTrump

Hillary Clinton should have been prosecuted and should be in jail.
Instead she is running for president in what looks like a rigged
election

8:23 AM · Oct 15, 2016

36,426 RETWEETS   **85,461** LIKES

 **Donald J. Trump** ✓
@realDonaldTrump

HILLARY FAILED ALL OVER THE WORLD. #BigLeagueTruth
✗LIBYA
✗SYRIA
✗IRAN
✗IRAQ
✗ASIA PIVOT
✗RUSSIAN RESET
✗BENGHAZI
#DrainTheSwamp

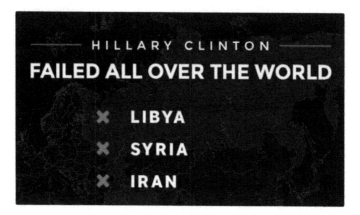

10:16 PM · Oct 19, 2016 from University of Nevada, Las Vegas

11,427 Retweets   **20,781** Likes

133

Donald J. Trump @
@realDonaldTrump

Crooked Hillary should not be allowed to run for president. She deleted 33,000 e-mails AFTER getting a subpoena from U.S. Congress. RIGGED!

8:01 AM · Nov 1, 2016

23,411 Retweets   **58,799** Likes

Donald J. Trump ✔
@realDonaldTrump

So terrible that Crooked didn't report she got the debate questions from Donna Brazile, if that were me it would have been front page news!

10:14 AM · Nov 1, 2016

32,232 Retweets   **79,640** Likes

Donald J. Trump ✓
@realDonaldTrump

WikiLeaks emails reveal Podesta urging Clinton camp to 'dump' emails.
Time to #DrainTheSwamp!

WikiLeaks emails reveal John Podesta urging Hillary Clinton camp to &#
washingtontimes.com

5:57 PM · Nov 1, 2016 from Eau Claire, WI

14,097 Retweets   **25,416** Likes

 **Donald J. Trump** ✔
@realDonaldTrump

TODAY WE MAKE AMERICA GREAT AGAIN!

6:43 AM · Nov 8, 2016

339,256 Retweets   **568,125** Likes